MW01226367

NOAH'S ARK

Let's Think About This

Written by

J. ALAN GROGG

Published by

JAG Publishing

ISBN-13: 9781544960340

ISBN-10: 1544960344

INTRODUCTION

Let's think about Noah's Ark and the great flood of the bible, breaking things down to try to understand if it is possible for a family of eight to build a boat large enough to load, transport, feed, and care for all the dry land species on the planet, for an entire year and then some. Let's take into account, the actual construction of the ark, the crews ability to build the ark, the ages of Noah and his family, the amount of precipitation that it would have taken to flood the earth, what it might have looked like when the earth was flooded, and after the waters receded, and the possibility that this one family could reproduce after the flood and repopulate the entire human species.

TABLE OF CONTENTS

CHAPTER ONE
GREAT FLOODS?

Let's think about Noah's Ark and the great flood and try to determine how we came to know this story and whether or not this story could possibly be true; and to try to determine whether or not it was the only flood story ever written about.

To begin with, one of the biggest problems with the story of Noah's Ark and the great flood is that, it is in fact, not the only flood story involving an angry god(s), a lot of rain, and a man that was given the honor of building and loading a boat full of animals before a flood hit, and then repopulating the world with his family.

If we listen to theists, they will claim that their version of the great flood is the right one and all the other great flood stories are myths.

According to the bible, several thousands of years ago, the biblical God was so angry at man, whom he had created, whom he could not control, and whom he could not get to listen to what he wanted from them, that he sent down a deadly flood to kill off the entire world population and start over with one family, and two of each species on earth.

Noah's Ark

"And the Lord said, I will destroy man whom I have created from the face of the earth; both man, and beast, and the creeping thing, and the fowls of the air; for it repenteth me that I have made them" *Genesis 6:7*

I guess God was pretty mad, to be a loving God and all!

Question: Why did God have to kill off everyone, including all the innocent women, children, and men, at the time, and not simply just focus on the ones who were being unruly and really needed to be eradicated from the planet?

After all that hard work God put in between Adam and Noah, and he just crumpled it up and threw it in the trash, instead of using an eraser to solve the problem.

Not too smart, and terrible logic!

Instead of fixing or eliminating all the broken people with the swish of a finger, or simply by just speaking it into happing, as theists claim God can do, God cast a spell of ruin among the entire earth's population and killed off everyone but Noah's family and some animals.

Wow! I guess that does prove he is a loving god!

What happened to thou shalt not kill?

If God is so powerful and almighty and able to do anything, how did he allow his people to get so out of control in the first place, and to the point to where he felt like he had to destroy all of them, good and bad?

I know! Theists will argue "free will," but that argument does not stand up to logic and scrutiny.

More on the reasons the "freewill" argument does not work, is covered in the book, "Creation" by J. Alan Grogg, available at Amazon.com and Kindle.

None the less, God sent down a great flood that lasted forty days and forty nights, killing every living land species on the planet except for the humans and animals that were on the ark.

With this one family, and a pair of each land species, God repopulated the world, and now, here we are.

Tada!

To theists, it is that simple. But, does that make their story true?

It's probably safe to say that most theists have never heard of the Epic of Gilgamesh, and for good reason.

Noah's Ark

I'm pretty sure they do not teach the Epic of Gilgamesh in the normal church settings because that would make it look like theists copied the story of Noah from the Epic of Gilgamesh.

I'm sure everyone knows the Christian religion does not plagiarize from other past religions! "Wink!"

The Epic of Gilgamesh is a story from ancient Mesopotamia, found to be one of the oldest known stories in human history.

This story was discovered in the mid 1800's, on a series of clay tablets dated back thousands of years, even before the time of the great flood of the bible.

The Epic of Gilgamesh consist of twelve tablets in which the eleventh tablet spoke about a great flood, very similar to the account of Noah's Ark which was written thousands of years later.

Hmm!

The flood story was included in the epic because in it the flood hero Utnapishtim was granted immortality by the gods, which fits the immortality theme of the Epic of Gildamesh.

In the story, Utnapishtim was granted eternal life which was to never again to be granted to anyone else.

The gods at that time, Anu, Enlil, Ninurta, Ennugi, and Ea were secretly planning a great flood that no one could know anything about.

One day while sitting in his house, Utnapishtim heard through a reed wall in his reed house, the god Ea, telling him about the god's flood plan, kind of like the Noah story.

Utnapishtim was told by Ea to destroy his house at all cost, and basically build a square boat, and load his relatives and craftsmen, and "all the beasts and animals of the field," kind of like the Noah story.

Of course, the gods went through with their plan and flooded the earth and mountains destroying all life on earth, kind of like in the Noah story.

When the water began to recede, Utnapishtim sent out birds to find land, kind of like the Noah story.

When the birds did not come back, Utnapishtim new there was dry land close by, which he eventually found, and there he released the animals into the wild and repopulated the world with his crew, and rebuilt the entire animal kingdom, kind of like the Noah story.

Noah's Ark

There are some differences between the Epic of Gilgamesh and the story of Noah's Ark.

For example: In the Epic of Gilgamesh, it only took the Semerian gods six days and nights to flood and flatten the earth, whereas it took the Christian God forty days and forty nights to do the same thing.

This proves that multiple gods are more efficient than one god!

Theists will likely try to argue that their story of Noah Story and the great flood was not plagiarized from the Epic of Gilgamesh.

OK! Maybe it wasn't!

Maybe the story of Noah was plagiarized from the Epic of Atra-Hasis which was written five hundred years before the Epic of Gilgamesh.

Or maybe it was even plagiarized from the flood myth of Ziusudra, which was before the Epic of Atra-Hasis.

Point is, that the story of Noah and the great flood, is only one of many stories of a great flood cause by angry gods, leaving one family to regenerate the world population.

Theists will likely claim that the story of Noah is real and all the other flood stories are only myths, yet they will never be able to justify or give any good reasons why their story is real and the others are false.

Sounds oddly like the theistic god claim!

These flood stories, that were written about before the time of the Noah's Ark story, that theists will claim are only myths, show a pattern that eerily resembles the pattern of the myths of other gods being worshiped, before the story of Jesus, in which some of those gods also had disciples, were born of virgin mothers, who were part of trinities, who had the attention of the magi, who had supernatural powers, and many more similarities.

Surely theists didn't plagiarize the whole damn bible, did they?

The only thing keeping us from truly answering that question of "who is right", is evidence, to which there is none to support any of these flood stories!

What makes theists believe the story of Noah is any more credible than the other great flood stories besides personal preference?

Answer: Nothing but doctrine. They are told to believe it!

7

Noah's Ark

After all, it only took a millennium to write about the story of Noah and the great flood after it supposedly happened.

Why so long?

Remember the old grade school assignment where the teacher tells one student a story, and by the time it gets to the last student, it is a completely different story?

Imagine what that would look like after a thousand years, if the flood had actually happened!

The truth is, there are many more great flood myths around the world than besides the ones mentioned in this text.

They are in almost every culture and every society, and to claim the story of Noah is the only correct one and the rest are false, is absurd!

And, to think any of them are true, at this point, is foolish!

The logical answer would be that since, not all of the great flood stories can be true, they are all likely false.

J. Alan Grogg

Noah's Ark

CHAPRER TWO
ONE FOR THE AGES

Let's think about the ages of Noah and his family, and how old they were when they began building the ark, and their ages once the ark was finished being built.

Let's also look to see if it was really possible that Noah and his family were able to repopulate the world, once the waters began to subside and Noah was able to find dry land.

According to the bible, Noah was around 500 years old when he began working on the ark, and he died when he was around 900 years old.

Have you ever wondered why man could live for hundreds of years in the bible, but most of us can't even live to be one hundred years old now, even though we are healthier now through scientific gains in medicine, lifestyles have changed making things easier to accomplish, we have more sanitary practices, and our life expectancy has grown by years, ever since man has been keeping age and life expectancy records?

Noah's Ark

Let's take the Noah story and their ages in for more questioning.

The claim that Noah was 500 years old when he began working on the ark is an absurd claim to begin with.

First of all, when was the last time you saw anyone over the age of 70 doing hard manual labor and not dying with a heart attack?

Answer: You probably haven't!

Let's ramp that up to 100 years of age and I will bet you a Snickers bar that you haven't at all!

Now, let's take someone doing hard manual labor at 500 years of age, for 100 consecutive years, minus Sundays of course because God would have killed them on the spot if they worked Sundays, and try to imagine what that would look like.

If a man could live to be 500 years old in the first place, he would likely drop dead at the sight of an axe or, at best, he may be able to still see the axe, but would likely not be able to pick it up.

And even more absurd is the claim that anyone that age could have cut down trees with primitive tools, trimmed them to size, carved them into the correct shapes, lifted them up and hammer them in place, etc. for 100 years (75-120 years), as the bible claims, and live through it.

Simply cutting wood is a very difficult task for a healthy 30-year-old now days, yet alone a 500 year old man.

Some theist will use the argument that God allowed man to live longer back then and they were healthier.

OK, then let's break that down.

Even if the bible says man lived longer back then, the claim does not take into account, the same gravity and body structure we still have to this day, meaning that man back then would still have to deal with the same aging process, the same bone structure and deterioration, illnesses, that were actually worse then, than they are now, accidental deaths, loss of motor skills, deterioration of eyesight, etc.

The odds are that it would be impossible to make it through the matrix long enough to live to be 500 years old, yet alone 1000 years for some, as the bible claims, and with seven other people making it there with you, is literally impossible because of what we do know about our bodies and gravity, and the aging process, through scientific studies, backed up by statistics.

This does not even include accidental risk factors, like logs falling on someone, or someone cutting an artery and possibly bleeding to death, or many other forms of wood working accidents that likely took the lives of, or, crippled man back in those days.

Geologist and scientists dig up skeletal remains of ancient humans all the time and are able to date their approximate age at the time of death by specific parameters used in forensic testing to date, that are consistently accurate, to today's skeletal remains that are examined during current day homicidal investigations, in which investigators know the age and gender of the victims.

Yet, we never hear of a dated ancient skeletal remain to be a person who was hundreds of years of age at the time of death.

Humans simply cannot live that long! Period!

In actuality, the current maximum human lifespan possible is considered to be 123 – 125 years of age.

That's higher now than it has ever been!

Let's face it and be real here, no matter what we do, no matter how good we take care of our bodies, our bodies eventually give out, and there is no way to avoid that living on this earth with the gravitational forces we have to contend with, in the conditions we live in, which are better now than they have ever been throughout the history of mankind.

The oldest know human to live that can be verified, was Jeanne Calment who lived to be 122 old.

There is no actual evidence that anyone has ever lived longer than that.

Jeanne Louise Calment (February 21, 1875 – August 4, 1997) was a French supercentenarian from Arles. She was the last person living to have personally met the artist, Vincent Van Gogh. Her lifespan has been thoroughly documented, with more proof of her age than for any other case.

There is a claim that Shirali Muslimov (1805 – 1973 (Allegedly), lived to be 168 years, however that claim cannot be verified with certainty. The only evidence of Muslimov's age is a passport that states his birth date in 1805. So, there could be some truth to it, however, what is more likely, is that he has been confused with someone else, possibly his father or grandfather.

Either way, neither of these examples come remotely close to some of the ages of man in the bible, including Noah, which weakens the story of Noah and the great flood.

Noah's Ark

In the developed countries of the 1700's, the fragmentary data that are available suggest that life expectancy at birth was around 35 to 40 years of age in the mid-1700s, and that number rose to about 45 to 50 years of age by the mid-1800s.

By the middle of the twentieth century life expectancy was approximately 66 to 67 years of age, and since the 1950 approximately eight more years have been added to life expectancy.

Point here is, that we are actually living longer now due to the scientific advances and medical practices that help us live longer, that were unavailable in the time of Noah.

Today, humans have better health care because of scientific discoveries and gains in medicines.

Because of science, many diseases have been eradicated from the planet since the time of Noah, and we live in more sanitary conditions now, compared to the time of Noah, simply because if what we do now know about bacteria, that people were unaware of during the time of Noah.

We can even look at today's earth population along with ancient data to show how it would be impossible for anyone to have lived much more than 100 years of age back in the time of Noah, if they could have even lived that long back then.

If we look at the chart of life expectancy at birth from the UN World Population Prospects of 2015, we find Hong Kong and China have the highest life expectancy including men and women, to be at 83.74 years of age, and at the bottom of the list at number 201, is the country of Swaziland, coming in last at 49.18 years of age life expectancy.

Unfortunately for the story of Noah, the region that most scholars believe Noah was from, Mesopotamia region of ancient Egypt, currently comes in number 120 out of 201 countries, with a life expectancy of 70.84 years.

Throughout ancient history, very little data was kept to verify the ages of people and how old they were when they died.

Some may have lived as long at 70 years of age, according to some account, however, In ancient Egypt, during the time of the Ptolemaic Period (320bc), people started documenting dates of births, dates of deaths and burials on tombstones, and dates of marriages.

Noah's Ark

These stats show that the average age of death during that period of time, for men and women combined, was 56 years of age with women living a little longer than man, as they still do today.

If we take the current age of life expectancy or that region of 70.84 years of age, and take away the 56 years of age that man in the same region lived in 320bc, it shows that life expectancy of that region has improved by 14.84 years in a little over 2300 years.

That is an improvement of .006 years, per year, of life expectancy in that region.

If we take the time between Noah (approx. 2000bc) and the Ptolemaic Period (320bc), and do the math, by using the age of 700 years, even though some claims are more, life expectancy went from 700 years of age to 56 years of age, meaning life expectancy dropped an average of .38 years, each year of life, for 1680 years, up to the Ptolemaic Period (320bc).

This is not perfect math, but I'm sure you get the point!

Now, we have to ask: What happened to make man lose .38 years of age, each and every single year, from the time of Noah, to the Ptolemaic Period (320bc)?

Most theists have never questioned this, however many theists will claim that the air was cleaner in the time of Noah.

If the theists claim was true that the air was cleaner back then, then what happened to the air to make man start losing .38 years of life, per year, up to the time of the Ptolemaic Period (320bc), and then, what changed to make life expectancy trend back upwards, to where man was gaining .006 years of life, per year up to modern the day?

When theists claim that the air was better in Noah's time, what does that look like? What did the air look like back then and what caused it to start being so bad to where man was losing so much of his life expectancy per year?

Many theists will try to use common sense here and point to air pollution and say, there, see!

That is what happened to the air; man polluted it!

The problem with this theory is that most of today's air pollution is from man-made resources such as vehicle emissions, industrial smoke stacks, aerosols, etc., things from the 20th century.

Through ice core examinations in South America, there is evidence of pollution from things like copper smelting operations from around 1400 B.C.E, however, those pollutant levels were nowhere close to the present-day pollution levels around the world.

This data would dismiss pollution as a cause of dying younger, because even with more pollution in the air today, we are living longer.

So, this would eliminate the "bad air" theory as a cause of losing .38 years of life per year, over a period of 2000 years.

Another theory theists use, is that sin causes man to live shorter lives now.

This is also contradictory because, according to the bible, man was living to be 700 to 900 years of age in the time of Noah, but things were so bad, because of all the sinning, that God destroyed all life on the planet accept for Noah's family and the animals on the ark.

Because of actual data that was kept from the Ptolemaic Period (320bc), through modern day statistics, we do know we are living much longer, yet, theists claim that man is sinning greater now than ever before, and Jesus is coming back very soon because of it. Kind of like before the great flood, but we do not hear of anyone living to be 700 years of age now.

Theists logic would suggest that if we lived longer back in Noah's day because of less sin, then we should be living shorter lives now days, because of all the sinning going on now, instead of gaining 14 year of age over the last 2000 years.

So, by being able to live to be 700 years of age, because we sinned less, to living to only 56 years of age, because we sinned more in the Ptolemaic Period, but now we are living 14 years longer now and are sinning even more, this dismisses the "sin theory" as a reason we do not live to be as old as Noah.

Some theists will also try to argue that man lived longer in the time of Noah because man was closer to God.

This is completely false because the Christian God was not even invented yet!

In the civilization of Samaria which scholars agree, started between 4500-4000bc, the Sumerians practiced a polytheistic religion, with anthropomorphic deities representing cosmic and terrestrial forces in their world.

During the middle of the 3rd millennium BCE, well before Christianity, the Sumerian deities became more anthropocentric and were "...nature gods transformed into city gods."

Noah's Ark

The earliest Sumerian literature of the 3rd millennium BC identifies four primary deities; Anu, Enlil, Ninhursag and Enki, but mentions nothing about a Christian God, and for good reason, Christianity had not been invented yet, and neither had their god!

From the Sumerian gods, came the Egyptian gods, which were prominent during the same time the Noah Story was to have occurred.

These gods were well documented on tombs and carvings, but still no mention of a Christian God.

So, even though there is no evidence to support the existence of any gods, we do have literature from before and after the time of Noah, that does mention multiple different gods, but nothing about the god mentioned in bible, and the story of Noah and the great flood.

This point alone dismisses the claim of a Christian god, which in turn, by default, dismissed the story of Noah.

However, if we can assume there was a Christian god back during the time of Noah and that same god still existed today, the theists claim that man was closer to God, therefor man lived longer back then, is still a false claim.

The bible makes claims of man living to be multiple of hundreds of years of age during and around the period of Noah, however, there is no actual evidence of that, but there is verifiable evidence from that period that man lived to be much closer to the age of man today.

If we tried using the theists logic that man lived longer due to being closer to God, then it would also suggest that the people who died very young, around the ages of 40 to 50 years of age, during the time of Noah, were likely not that close to God.

Let's think about that and how this analogy compares to today.

There are many people on earth who truly believe in Jesus and God, even without any evidence, however, none of these people come even close to living much longer than 100 years of age, ever, yet alone live to be 700 to 900 years of age, and they are "very close to God," and in fact, likely know more about Christian God than most people could have known back in the days of Noah who were able to live to be 700 years of age, supposedly, even if the Christian God had already been invented by then.

In fact, according to the Pew Research Center study on life expectancy by religious groups (2010 – 2015), Christians who are at

71 years of life expectancy, falls near the bottom half of life expectancy of religious groups, behind Jews (80), Unaffiliated (75), Buddhist (74), and folk religion (73), other religions (71), while Christians life expectancy is above Hindus (66) and Muslims (67).

This study also projects life expectancy to the year 2055, with Christians and Jews making the least growth in life expectancy at an additional 5 years, while the other groups were 6-8 additional years of life expectancy, by the year 2055.

Statistics show that countries with a high percentage of nonbelievers are among the freest, most stable, best-educated, and healthiest nations on earth.

When nations are ranked according to a human-development index, which measures such factors as life expectancy, literacy rates, and educational attainment, the five highest-ranked countries — Norway, Sweden, Australia, Canada, and the Netherlands — all have high degrees of nonbelief.

Of the fifty countries at the bottom of the index, all are intensely religious.

These facts not only make it very difficult for theists to argue, using man's relationship with God, as the reason man lived longer back in the period of Noah, but they in fact, actually disprove the claim.

So, by taking all the evidence into account, it is clear to see that the evidence points to the fact that man has never been able to live to be hundreds of years of age! Ever!

It simply cannot happen and there is absolutely no evidence to prove that it can, or that it has, no matter what you were taught and no matter how hard you want to believe it!

Not only does age have a corresponding effect on the physical human body, but it also has a corresponding effect on the reproductive organs of humans.

Because of the reproductive organs which lose their ability to function properly after certain ages, this alone puts damper on the hopes that the eight people on the boat could have repopulated the earth

If Noah's sons were equivalent to the age of father and sons' relationships now days, that would mean they were also nearly as old as Noah, not to mention all their wives being close to the same ages.

Can you even imagine a 700-year-old woman giving birth?

Through tons of lengthy scientific studies and data collecting, we know that the ideal age to have a baby is somewhere between 27 and 35 years of age, and we actually know why!

Giving birth beyond that range is possible, but the further away we get from that range, in either direction, the more at risk the pregnancy is, or the higher the risk of a child being born with developmental, mental, physical, or medical issues.

Nonbelievers do not believe in the bible or the story of Noah, but even if the bible were true, and since the bible does not mention anything about miraculous births by the women of the ark after the great flood, we have to conclude that the women would have aged and given birth by the same natural rules as women of that era did, which is not so different from today, although we do now have more sanitary places to give birth and better medical options for when we are sick, which in turn, help us to produce healthier offspring and to live longer.

When the authors of the bible wrote, and or plagiarized, the story of Noah and the great flood, and the repopulation of the world from Noah's family, the authors made a critical error by not at least trying to cover up their tracks by including miraculous acts of births from the ark story.

According to the Guinness book of world records, the oldest mother to give birth was Maria del Carmen Bousada Lara (Spain, b. 5 January 1940), who gave birth by caesarean section to twin boys, Christian and Pau, aged 66 years 358 days at the Sant Pau hospital, Barcelona, Spain on 29 December 2006.

A woman in India, Daljinder Kaur, who's believed to be at least 70 years old, gave birth to a son named Arman (meaning "wish" in Hindi) on April 19, 2016, however it is unclear if her age has been verified.

There are other births by mothers in their 50's and 60's, but they are very rare because reproductive organs normally wear down and stop working by these ages, almost always, due to the fact that age-related fertility problems increase after this age.

Healthy women in the age range of 27 to 35 years of age, usually have it pretty easy when it comes to pregnancy; it's no wonder they have the most babies!

Most births in this group are often conceived within about two months of trying, and have a relatively low risk of miscarriage and they have the fewest medical complications during pregnancy.

The risk of Down syndrome or other chromosomal birth defects are lower for this age group of mothers.

Women ages 20 to 24 have a slightly higher risk of preeclampsia, a dangerous pregnancy condition that causes high blood pressure and protein in the urine.

Doctors are unsure why some women get preeclampsia, and the condition is a serious one, because It can lead to a slowdown of fetal growth and preterm delivery.

Women in their early 20s also have a greater chance of having a low birth weight baby, largely because of poor health habits.

Young women are also more likely to have a poor diet, delay prenatal care, and gain less than the recommended amount of weight all of which increase the risk of having a baby who is underweight.

Most women 35 and older have healthy babies, but studies suggest that they may have more problems along the way, because fertility begins to decrease more rapidly after age 35, making it harder to conceive.

According to statistics from the American Society for Reproductive Medicine, about one-third of women older than 35 have issues with fertility.

Women in this age group are also more likely to suffer a miscarriage than younger women. In fact, a recent Danish study discovered that more than 20 percent of pregnant women ages 35 to 39 miscarried, whereas miscarriages for women between 27 and 35 years of age is around 10%.

Women older than 35 are also more likely to have problems such as preeclampsia, diabetes, premature birth, and a low birth weight baby, as well as placental problems during pregnancy.

Women over 40 year of age have a harder time conceiving a baby with more than 50 percent have difficulties conceiving at all.

The two risks that increase most markedly in your 40s are chromosomal abnormalities, such as Down's with a risk of one in 100 at age 40 and one in 30 at age 45, and miscarriage risk of about 50% by the age of 42.

Women at this age are also almost three times as likely to develop diabetes during pregnancy than moms in their 20s, along with delivery risk, and fetal distress,

Menopause is a normal condition that all women experience as they age.

The term "menopause" can describe any of the changes a woman goes through either just before or after she stops menstruating, marking the end of her reproductive period.

For men, semen counts gradually deteriorate over the years, and according to An American Journal of Gynecology study, the odds for age-related male infertility increase each year, and the chance of getting your partner pregnant drop 11 percent with each passing year after age 40.

The study also shows that while age-related male infertility may not prevent you from impregnating your partner, as sperm ages, genetic changes (mutations) may occur on a more frequent basis.

This leads to an increase in the number of chromosomally abnormal sperm, which tend to not be able to fertilize an egg with the same efficiency as chromosomally normal sperm.

On rare occasions, abnormal sperm do fertilize an egg, potentially leading to a greater risk for some of the following health disorders in the offspring of men over the age of 40: apert's syndrome, autism, recurrent miscarriage, and schizophrenia.

Could you imagine a world where a majority of people have severe mental health and developmental issues?

So, besides women, there are issues with men over 40 years of age, having children; not to mention men over 500 years of age, which would greatly complicate the repopulation agenda, and at best, produce a world of serious mental health issues, which in turn would prevent man from ever being capable of rebuilding the world ever again.

So, if we honestly take the age of the crew into consideration when building the ark and repopulating the world, it is clear to see that it would be literally impossible, and therefore be another solid reason to dismisses the story of Noah and the great flood.

But, then we get into the issue of inbreeding to repopulate the earth's population, because of the bloodline between Noah and his sons.

Through scientific discoveries we have found that having children within the same family (inbreeding), comes with a high risk, which can cause genetic disorders and mutations among the offspring produced from the same family bloodlines mating.

The definition of inbreeding is "the production of offspring from the mating or breeding of individuals or organisms that are closely related genetically. By analogy, the term is used in human reproduction, but more commonly refers to the genetic disorders and other consequences that may arise from incestuous sexual relationships and consanguinity. Inbreeding results in homozygosity, which can increase the chances of offspring being affected by recessive or deleterious traits. This generally leads to a decreased biological fitness of a population, called inbreeding depression, which is its ability to survive and reproduce." *Source: Wikipedia*

So, on top of the issue of the age of the crew having babies, then add on top of that, the issues with inbreeding, and it would be literally impossible to ever reproduce a productive civilization, ever again.

CHAPTER THREE
THE RAIN

Let's think about the amount of rain it would have taken to cover the earth to the mountain tops, as claimed in the bible, and see if it is literally possible.

In Genesis, it says the highest mountains are covered with water during the great flood, and even a little higher just to make sure the job was done.

This poses a bit of a problem with the story of Noah and the great flood because the amount of rain it would have taken to fill the earth to the highest mountain top in the world, which is Mount Everest, which stands at 29,000 feet above sea level, is literally impossible.

Let's start by breaking this down to determine how much rain it would have actually taken.

If we take the height of Mount Everest, which is 29,000 feet above sea level, we can convert that to inches by multiplying 29,000' by 12", which would equal 348,000"of water to reach the peak of Mount Everest.

To put that into perspective, the current average total rainfall worldwide is 39" per year.

If we took the total number of inches of rain it would have taken to flood the earth (348,000"), as claimed in the bible, at the normal rain rate per year, it would have taken 9823 years to collect the same amount of rain that fell in 40 days and 40 nights according to the bible.

Now if we take that 348,000" of water and divide that by the amount of days it rained during the great flood, which was 40 days, this would equal 8700" of rain per day.

Now let's break that down by the number of hours in a day, which is 24 hours.

That equals 363" of rain each hour, for 40 straight days.

We can break that down even further into minutes, by dividing by 60 minutes, and we get 6" of rain per minute.

Can anyone even try to imagine what that would even look like?

Think about it!

It would have taken it raining at a rate of 6" each minute, for 40 days and 40 nights, to reach the top of Mount Everest.

Let's put that into perspective once more.

The greatest 24-hour rainfall recorded on earth occurred on Reunion Island at the site of Foc-Foc on January 7-8, 1966 when 71.85" of rainfall was measured during Tropical Storm Denise.

That would come to an average of about 2.99" of rain each hour for 24 straight hours, or .05" of rain each minute.

This amount, of the greatest recorded rainfall in a 24 hour period, 71.85", would have fallen in twelve minutes during the great flood of the bible, according to the bible timeline claims.

The greatest official total of rainfall for a 48 hour period is 98.15" at Cherrapunji, India that fell on June 15-16, 1995.

That would have taken about sixteen minutes to fall according to the bible stats.

This would make the great flood stats 118 times heavier than the heaviest rainfall ever recorded on earth.

That's a pretty substantial difference; and for 40 days and 40 nights without letup! And people actually believe this?

There have been other unofficial reports of more rain falling within a 24 and 48 hour period, but nothing even remotely close to what it would have taken to flood the entire earth in 40 days and 40 nights.

Let's look at this a different way.

I'm sure most of you have seen tropical storms and hurricanes either in person and or on TV.

They are both basically the same kind of storm, only separated in name, by wind speeds, but both carry a substantial amount of rain in them.

Most of us know what a hurricane looks like on radar, as it is basically a 300 mile wide tornado with very dense cloud ring with an eye in the middle.

As you may know, hurricanes are very intense and relentless and if you have ever been in a hurricane, or even a tropical storm, you likely found it to be a very frightening, very destructive, and a very dangerous event.

Now, let's make that storm 118 times denser than the most intense storm ever recorded, with 118 times more precipitation than the most intense storm ever recorded, and 118 more times ferocious than the most intense storm ever recorded, and place this storm over the entire earth, at one time, and continue this earth enveloping storm for 40 days and 40 nights with no relief.

With this much precipitation, almost everyone would have likely drowned in the first hours, and the rest would have likely died shortly after by all the churning of the water, not to mention being electrocuted by all the lightning that would have been present with all the friction of the clouds.

Another thing that doesn't make much logical sense is, that God shouldn't have needed to make it rain for 40 days and nights to kill all the people on earth, including the people in the high terrains, because the amount of rain falling during the great flood event, would have been like standing under Niagara Falls, so the people living in the mountains would have drowned pretty quickly simply by the amount of rain that was falling, according to the bible.

With this much precipitation falling, every structure would have quickly been destroyed by the sheer weight of the rain hitting all at once, along with every tree, plant, bush, etc.

Every bit of soil on earth would have been washed down from every mountain, leaving nothing but exposed rocks as one would observe at the bottom of any waterfall, and every bit of land sediment would basically be the same level around the entire earth as it settled in after the storm.

Noah's Ark

This would mean that no current land would rise above any other land, but only rock would rise above all the soil, which is obviously not the case as we have land terrain 1000 to 2000' above sea level, and higher at some points, which should have been washed away if the flood would have happened.

Most of us understand what a hurricane does to the seas, causing them to be very violent and deadly, and non-navigable.

Now, try to imagine Noah's Ark in these heavily churning seas for 40 days and 40 nights, constantly with no relief.

How could anyone or any animal on a boat, ever stand up, sit still, use the bathroom, eat or drink, feed the animals, even sleep, when they would have had to constantly hang on and brace themselves for dear life for 40 days straight?

There would have been no smooth sailing at all, unless God somehow hovered the ark high above the clouds for 40 days while he destroyed the earth.

However, that claim is not in the bible, so we have to conclude that Noah's Ark was floating on the waters, as most boats do.

There would have been no calm waters to take a break from all the tossing around by the waters, and mere exhaustion would have killed the people on board along with most animals within that 40 days.

This would have been like the most extreme nonstop theme park ride ever, for 40 straight days.

No human body or animal could have withstood the relentless forces for that long of period of time.

So, for there to have been this much rain, for this long of period of time, and for a boat, and or the passengers and animals to have survived this very violent and relentless storm, would have been impossible!

Another problem with the amount of rain that had to fall during the great flood, as described in the bible, is how rain actually forms.

As most people may know, rain is condensation in our atmosphere that eventually falls in the form of rain or snow, and sometimes hail.

What most people may not know, is the properties of the rain as it is formed high above the earth and what it actually takes for rain to form, and eventually fall.

Noah's Ark

Water requires a non-gaseous surface to make the transition from a vapour to a liquid; this process is called condensation.

You may have noticed something similar on a glass of cold lemonade during the summer when the outside of the glass condensates, or becomes wet, by collecting water vapours in the air which cling to the colder glass surface.

In the rain clouds, small particles from dust, clay, soot, black carbon from grassland or forest fires, sea salt from ocean wave spray, soot from factory smokestacks or internal combustion engines, sulfate from volcanic activity and even pollution provide surfaces for water vapours in the atmosphere to condense.

These vapours can even cling to other moisture droplets in the sky in the right conditions.

The vapours condense on these particles and together they form clouds, and when the clouds become saturated enough and can no longer hold the rain, they being to fall on earth as rain.

Taking the cold glass of lemonade to explain this in much simpler terms, the cold glass is equivalent to a giant "particle" in the sky in which the water vapours can stick to (condensate) forming droplets of water, and we can then call the glass, a cloud.

When too much condensation builds up on the glass or particle, it begins to drip down the side of the glass, like the rain falling from the clouds.

So, to make rain, we have to have several components, including water vapour, particles in the atmosphere, and the temperature has to be warm enough at the surface to make these vapours rise, and the air has to be cold enough to cause the vapours to condensate, or cling to a particle.

During the great flood, as heavy as it had to rain for the 40 days and 40 nights, there would have been very little opportunity for moisture to continue pouring out of the clouds to produce that amount of rain for that length of time.

The vapours and particles would have had to keep rising and condensing rapidly enough to keep the rains coming as hard as they did, as long as they, according to the bible data.

This would have been literally impossible.

After a short while into the storm, the particles needed to cause rain, would have not been able to become airborne long enough to climb to the altitude to where the air is colder, meaning there would be no more particles for water vapours to cling to.

The amount of rain falling would have prevented these particles and water vapours, from being able to rise in the first place, which in turn, would have prevented any particles or vapours from climbing high enough to participate in the condensation process, meaning there would be no more rain available to fall.

The amount of rain falling during the storm would have also likely stabilized the air temperature enough to interfere with the condensation process and therefore no more rain drops could have formed.

So, this would lead us to the question: Where did all that rain come from?

Since we know what rain is, and how it forms, the story of Noah and the great flood is severely flawed, at best!

Some theists may claim that clouds do rise above Mount Everest and therefor can produce rain at that altitude.

Yes, it is true that some clouds sometimes do rise above the altitude of Mount Everest, however most of these clouds are lightweight clouds of crystals which cannot produce rain.

Some thunderheads can climb as high as 50,000 feet, however conditions have to be right for this to happen including changes in air temperatures meeting and colliding, and moisture that is able to climb and build with the cloud to produce this height of cloud.

However, the rain falls from the bottom the cloud where it is warmer, and any condensation that may fall above the level of 32 degrees, will likely fall as frozen precipitation till it reaches a temperature above 32 degrees before it begins turning into liquid.

This means that if the water rose to the bottom of this thunder head cloud, and kept rising, high into the atmosphere, the rain would eventually turn into frozen precipitation.

Clouds are classified into four basic categories, depending largely on the height of their bases above the ground.

High-level clouds, called cirrus clouds, can reach heights of 20,000 feet and are typically thin. They do not produce rain and often indicate fair weather. They are usually made up of ice.

Midlevel clouds form between 6,500 feet and cirrus level. They themselves sometimes produce virga, which is rain or snow that does not reach the ground.

Low-level clouds lie below 6,500 feet. Meteorologists refer to them as stratus clouds. They're often dense, dark, and rainy (or snowy) though they can also be cottony white clumps interspersed with blue sky.

Noah's Ark

The most dramatic types of clouds are cumulus and cumulonimbus, or thunderheads. Rather than spreading out in bands at a fairly narrow range of elevations, like other clouds, they rise to dramatic heights, sometimes well above the level of transcontinental jetliner flights.

Cumulus clouds are fair-weather clouds. When they get big enough to produce thunderstorms, they are called cumulonimbus.

These clouds are formed by upwelling plumes of hot air, which produce visible turbulence on their upper surfaces, making them look as though they are boiling.

As thunderheads reach high elevations, their tops encounter high winds that cause them to spread out sideways, earning them the nickname "anvil tops." They can reach elevations of 50,000 feet.

These are the clouds, that would have been necessary in order for it to have rained like it needed to rain, for 40 days and 40 nights, in order to meet the flood level claims, according to the bible.

Some may say, what about hurricanes? They produce of a lot of rain too and reach the heights of the cumulonimbus clouds.

The problem with hurricanes is that they are water creatures, generating more intensity while moving across warm water.

Once the hurricane reaches land fall, it quickly begins to dissipate because of the lack of water to regenerate.

This leave us no other option but to consider the cumulonimbus clouds as the clouds that produced all that rain in the great flood story, however, these clouds could have never produced that much precipitation for that long of period of time, and the amount that would have been needed to cover the entire earth.

Even with a combination of hurricanes filling the oceans and the cumulonimbus clouds covering dry land, this could not be possible because of the ingredients needed to make it rain that hard for that length of time.

The lifespan of these clouds are too short, as if they have a safety shut off of shorts.

Cumulonimbus storm cells can produce torrential rain of a convective nature.

Most storm cells die after about 20 minutes, when the precipitation causes more downdraft than updraft, causing the energy to dissipate.

If there is enough solar energy in the atmosphere, however, the moisture from one storm cell can evaporate rapidly, resulting in a new cell forming just a few miles from the former one.

This can cause thunderstorms to last for several hours, but not continuously for 40 days and 40 nights. Cumulonimbus clouds are most common in tropical regions, meaning the entire earth would have to be warm or of a tropical nature for this to occur world-wide.

This would mean the ice caps would have to thaw out quickly before the great flood, and unfortunately, scientists have never found this to have happened in the ice cap cores they have studied.

These ice caps, have layers that resemble tree rings, making it fairly easy for scientists to determine the age of glaciers within a fair degree of confidence.

Ice glaciers are dated back beyond the time of Noah, and show that, at least in the polar regions, there was no evidence of any quick thaw or flood, meaning that other warm regions on earth would have had to make up for those areas of the earth surface that did not meet the tropical ingredients of a rain storm, and the polar ice caps would have been unaffected somehow by the great flood, which would have been impossible since they are well below the height of Mount Everest.

Just as it takes heat to evaporate water from the surface of the Earth, which allows the water vapour to rise, heat is released when water condenses to form clouds.

In general, cumulonimbus require moisture, an unstable air mass, and a lifting force (heat) in order to form.

Cumulonimbus clouds typically go through three stages: the developing stage, the mature stage (where the main cloud may reach supercell status in favorable conditions), and the dissipation stage.

The average thunderstorm has a 15 mile radius, and depending on the conditions present in the atmosphere, these three stages take an average of about 30 minutes to go through.

Lines of thunderstorms can reproduce these clouds for the life of the front, however, it is impossible for these clouds to form everywhere on earth, at the same time, and continue to reproduce heavy rain for 40 days and 40 nights because all the ingredients needed to make it rain could not sustain themselves if that much precipitation was falling for that long of period of time.

Heat from the sun is one of the biggest ingredients needed to make it rain, and the rain alone would have quickly dissipated most of that, simply by blocking the sun's heat from further assisting with the formation of rain.

The problem with the story of Noah and the great flood is that in order for it to rain as much as the bible claims it did, the total earth would have to be engulfed with cumulonimbus clouds and that is literally impossible because of the various regions of the planet with some regions being favorable to produce the conditions needed, and other regions that could never produce these conditions.

The entire earth would have had to have had the right ingredients and the right conditions, all at the same time, which would have been literally impossible because of the dynamics involved in producing rain and how our weather works.

Since we know through science, how rain clouds actually do work, this eliminates clouds as a possible source for all the rain it would have taken to flood the earth.

So, in order for there to be enough water to flood the earth to the height of Mount Everest, would mean that the water had to come from somewhere else, and with little options, space would have had to be the resource.

If you can imagine what it would be like with that same amount of water, that was needed to flood the earth, 29,000' of it worldwide, surrounding the earth, above the altitude of Mount Everest before it fell, and from what science does know about our atmospheric temperatures, every bit of that precipitation would have been of the frozen variety, and therefore, would it would have not have been able to fall as liquid, but would have instead, been a cover of 29,000' of solid ice, eventually causing the earth to freeze from the outside down to the core.

So, by using science and our knowledge of how weather actually works, and by using basic math, it is literally impossible for the earth to have flooded to the height of Mount Everest.

Not only does the math and science of rain disprove the flood story of the bible, but there are no geological records to prove the world was ever flooded, as claimed in the bible.

Noah's Ark

The earth is covered in layers of sediment and rock, and as land masses push together to form mountains, and as land masses drift apart, they expose these layers of rock and sediment which can be studied by scientists.

From what we do know about current day flood studies, and the effect they have on geography, carving out the land and moving sediment and debris; if a global flood would have occurred, there should be plenty of evidence of this seen in the geological studies, however, to date, there is none!

Not only is there no geological evidence of a great flood, some cultures and civilizations apparently made it through the great flood uninterrupted.

I guess they didn't get the memo!

So, by the evidence we do have, that there is no geological evidence showing a global flood has ever happened, and with several civilizations apparently unaffected by and or not taking part in the great flood, and the lack of ingredients available to make enough rain to make the great flood even possible, the story of the great flood of the bible proves to be clearly made up, or even worse, plagiarized from an earlier culture, and sold by Christians to gullible people as another divine act from the invisible man in the sky.

Noah's Ark

CHAPTER FOUR
LOGISTICS

Let's think about the logistics and how things might have looked when the ark was being loaded with animals, people, supplies, and necessities.

Zoologist have claimed there to be over one million dry land species in the world, and some estimates are between three and thirty million species, including non-discovered species which may take that to a much higher number.

But, for the sake of this argument, let's take one million species, including mammals, reptiles, birds, insects, etc. and go with that to make this point, even though the number would actually be higher.

Theists will use apologetic theories of how to get these numbers down to more manageable numbers and for good reason.

Even theists have enough common sense to understand that there is no logical way the ark could have carried two of every species, clean and unclean animals, seven pairs of every kind of bird, and two of all creatures that move along the ground, male and female, for 40 days and 40 nights, only being cared for by eight people, and still making it through the journey alive.

Estimates are that there are currently 10,500 species of birds alone. If we cut that in half back to the time of the great flood, that would be 5250 different species of birds. Times that by 7 as God commanded, that would be no less than 36,750 birds on the ark, during a terrible storm, meaning every single one of them would have to roost during the storm for 40 days and 40 nights, inside the ark. Where did all these birds roost? And, where did all the droppings go?

And just to add, if the bird species was close to 5250 species, during the time of Noah, and today there are 10,500 different species, then that would be a point for evolution. And everyone knows how theists hate that word! Otherwise the ark would have to carried over 70,000 birds.

So, which is it theists? Is the story of Noah severely flawed, at best, or is evolution real? Or, both?

Funny thing is, if theists would concede that evolution is real, which some actually do, it would actually help make the story of Noah a little more believable as far as the number of species that actually needed to ride along on the ark, in order to keep the hopes of future species alive.

This number of one million different species, does not even account for the one million plant species that would have to had to of been carried on the ark so that the crew could plant and regrow the vegetation because the earths vegetation would have been destroyed by the flood, and therefore it would have had to be replanted and cultivated in order to keep millions of species alive once the ark did make it to dry land.

After all, most plants cannot stay under water for that length of time and survive, especially with that amount of destruction that would have uprooted and fatally soaked each dry land plant.

In the meantime while plants were growing and reproducing more plants, what would the herbivores eat to stay alive while the vegetation grew plentiful enough for them to begin feeding on them without eating what's left of a certain vegetation species?

Due to the length of time needed for fruits and vegetables to grow and produce, how would Noah and his crew survive without the critical vitamins needed from the fruits and vegetables.

Noah's Ark

The question of vegetation survival from the great flood opens up an entirely different argument, so we will leave it for now and move on with the current topic.

When loading one million different species on the ark, all in one day, as the bible claims, this means that eleven pairs of species would have to enter the ark, every second, for that entire 24 hour period, to get them all in the ark before the rain began to fall.

Even if there were multiple ramps to load the different species, the total number of species would make it very difficult to organize and load the ark that efficiently and logically.

Not only would loading a million species in one day be an impossible task, even if they were all insects, but having room for each species would be an even bigger problem because many of them would require separate housing from other species because of instinctive behavioral characteristics that may be harmful to other species on the ark.

With the ark being 450' long, 75' wide, and 45'tall.

If we use math here, with the ark having 1,518,750 cubic feet, not counting the inside structures, levels, and beams that take up more space, and divide out the space equally among all species, that would mean that each species, a pair of two each, would have to share 1.5 cubic foot of boat space.

Not floor space, but cubic space (1.5' tall x1.5' wide x1.5' depth).

That's not much room! And, that's counting top to bottom, front to back, and side to side, of the ark.

If we take out the space needed for more levels with additional flooring, and the beams needed to support all this weight, the amount of cubic foot space reduces even more.

Later in this text we will discuss how the available space for housing all the different species on the ark would actually, in reality, likely have been considerably lower, if the story was true.

Yes, there are small dry land species that would not take up much space, however, the bigger species such as elephants, giraffes, hippos, cows, horses, etc. would take up vast amounts of space quickly with the average size of animals being about the size of a sheep, which alone would take up several cubic feet each.

This does not even include room for the crew, and food and supplies it would have taken to keep eight humans and a million species alive for 40 days and nights.

But, for the sake of argument, let's say that Noah and his family were somehow able to load that many species on the ark in one day, and they managed to set sail for the new world.

Oops! Wrong story!

But, even if they were able to load all these species, and set afloat in the great flood, feeding each species regularly would be an even greater task and could possibly be the final nail in the coffin of the Noah story and the great flood.

If we do the math, feeding two million creatures a minimum of once each day would be the same exact math used in loading the ark.

In order to keep the million species alive, Noah and his crew would have to feed 11 different species every single second of every day and night, for 40 days and 40 nights to keep the species healthy and alive.

This would be a tough task even if all the species were insects or rodents.

If we broke that down by crew member, that would mean each crew member would have to feed 1.3species every second of every day for 40 days and nights.

Yet, if we broke that down to even more reasonable numbers, as theists try to do, we could take only the mammals and reptiles, to which there are approximately 13,000 species.

These alone would require the crew to feed one species every nine seconds around the clock.

Of, course the rest of the land species would perish along with all the insect creatures needed for a healthy eco system, meaning the eco system would not be able to function properly causing some of the species that did make the journey, to die once the crew stopped feeding them.

Think about that! Look around you now and try to do one different thing, every nine second, whether it is picking up a pen every nine seconds, moving your mouse every nine seconds, even simply just making a movement every nine second.

Some theists will claim that some species, would not have had to get on the ark, because they could have floated on debris during the storm.

This is incorrect for two reasons!

First of all, that would have gone against what God commanded, that "all" the species be on the ark, not on driftwood.

Noah's Ark

The second issue is that as hard as it had to rain for 40 days and 40 nights, you might as well have put these species in a pickle jar full of water and closed the lid because they would have drowned, period, with as much rain as it would have taken to flood the earth in that amount of time, and as hard as it would have had to rain during that time; like being under Niagara Falls.

As we know, most animals and dry land species eat multiple times each day, and a lack of food would cause weakness and illnesses, and even death for some species if the crew was unable to feed them multiple times a day.

If we take the logistics of all the food and water that had to be loaded onto the ark, that would have been necessary in order to feed the animals for 40 days and 40 nights, not only would that have taken up very valuable space, but simply feeding every species would have been an impossible feat.

The crew would have also had to keep extras of some species alive during the entire voyage, as food for the predatorial animals.

This would have taken up even more space and more of the crew's time just feeding the critters that would have eventually been eaten during the journey.

To decrease some of this inventory space in order to try to make more sense of this story, some theists will say that the crew could have gotten water from the falling rain, but if the ark was sealed, that would not have been possible, and for as hard as it had to rain to flood the earth in 40 days, if there were even a very small opening in the ark for rain water, the ark would have flooded quickly.

When we look at the amount of space that was available on the ark, we can take the elephant for example to see how quickly space can shrink.

Not only does an elephant take up an enormous amount of cubic space, elephants are high maintenance when it comes to food and water.

The African elephants can eat as much as 600 pounds of food a day, and drink as much as 50 Gallons of water.

Even if we cut that in half for smaller elephants, and count the food and water needed for the pair of that species for a year float, the ark would need to transport 219,000 pounds of food, which is 109.50 tons, just for the two small elephants.

To put that into perspective, that would be the equivalent of 5 current day, standard shipping containers, which are 20' in length, by 8'6" wide, by 7'9.25" in height.

The ark would also have to transport 18250 gallons of fresh drinking water for the pair of elephants to have enough water to drink in a year. That would equal another 3 current day standard shipping containers.

That's a total of 8 shipping containers the ark would have had to transport just for two of the smaller elephants.

To put all of this into perspective, one current day 20' shipping container contains 1360 cubic foot of inventory.

If we take the 8 containers needed for the feeding supplies for the two elephants on the ark, and multiply that by 1360 cubic feet each, that equals, 10,880 cubic feet of space needed just for the food and drinking supply for two elephants, not to mention the cubic feet needed for their physical bodies.

Remember, the average cubic space available for each species, is 1.5 cubic feet per species, and the elephant's food took up 10,000 cubic feet all by itself.

The amount of space, taken away by the additional floors and beams, assuming there were multiple levels, and just two elephants and their food, leaves a lot less room for the remaining 999,999 species, yet alone the food for the remaining species, and the crew.

Noah and his family would have been extremely busy keeping all the species alive, in extremely crowded conditions, while the bird dropping were constantly raining down on all living creatures on the ark.

When would Noah and his family ever have time to eat, sleep, use the bathroom, etc.?

Some theists may claim that God took care of Noah's family and all the animals, keeping them fed and healthy while they were on the boat.

If this were true, that would pose a bit of an issue with the loving god claim, because if God can keep a family of eight and a boat full of animals healthy for 40 days and 40 nights, then why doesn't he keep everyone on earth healthy all the time, instead of killing all of them?

The fact is, if there were a god who could keep a family of eight and two million creatures alive for 40 days and 40 nights, and cause enough rain to flood the entire world, then that same god should have had the power and or ability to keep man under his control better, instead of allowing man become unruly to the point to where he felt like he had to kill them all by drowning.

This would be a pathetic god at best!

By the way, how did animals like kangaroos, penguins, and polar bears make it to the ark from Australia, the north pole, and the Antarctica? And, how were they able to get back after the flood?

Now that would have been an impressive journey!

One final critical error with the logistics of the Noah story is the wellbeing of all the aquatic species.

Yes, fish can survive in water, that is true, however different fish require different water environments and ecosystems to survive.

Salt water fish require the salt waters of the oceans to survive, while fresh water fish require fresh waters from lakes and rivers to survive.

Some aquatic creatures also require water systems that have a higher amount of pressure due to living under the pressures of the deep oceans, while some species require very shallow waters to survive.

A storm of this magnitude would have completely destroyed every kind of water system in the world, mixing salt water and fresh water, and changing temperatures of the waters, which is so critical to so many species, which in turn would have likely killed most aquatic species during the flood.

Because of this much diversity in the water systems of our planet, Noah and his crew would have had to of built fish tanks, some very specialized with pressures and special lighting, and carry two of every water species on the planet on the ark.

And, let's not forget about the room that would be needed on board the ark for aquatic vegetation.

This issue of the aquatic species, neglected by God and Noah, only complicate the story of Noah the great flood, and in actuality, actually smashes the story of Noah and the great flood into tiny little pieces!

We could go on here but I think you probably get the point by now.

Theists will always use apologetics to try to make the Noah story work by bending and twisting the fairytale to make some people believe that it really happened.

Noah's Ark

When a contradiction is pointed out, theists will usually make a different unjustified claims, to try to cover up the contradictions of the bible, when in reality, these cover-up claims, make theists look even more foolish than if they were to simply stick to what the bible appears to say and simply claim "faith," as they do with everything else in the bible that doesn't make any logical sense.

There is no logical sense with the story of Noah and the great flood, so why try to make other nonsensical and fallacious claims to cover up the garbage?

In reality, the logistics alone, should be enough to discredit the story of Noah and the great flood, while at the same time putting the god claim in serious doubt, because if the great flood doesn't happen, the bible falls apart!

CHAPTER FIVE
COOL WORLD

Let's think about what things would have looked like if the story of Noah and the great flood were true and the Ark did make it to day 40, floating high above the tallest mountains.

First of all, we would have to understand what the weather conditions would like be at the altitude of the summit of Mount Everest, because that is the highest point above sea level in the world.

This would give us a good idea of what Noah and his family had to look forward to once God flooded the earth, higher than Mount Everest.

One of the biggest problems that goes back to the rain and condensation, is the temperature of our atmosphere at the altitude of Mount Everest which is too cold to produce anything other than frozen precipitation.

Nearly everyone knows water begins to freeze at thirty-two degrees Fahrenheit.

In order for it to rain, or, in order for frozen precipitation to turn into rain, the air temperatures have to be above freezing, or thirty-two degrees Fahrenheit, otherwise the precipitation will fall as frozen precipitation, and not as rain drops, which is what it would take to flood the earth.

Of course, some of this precipitation can start off as snow or ice and melt as it gets closer to the ground where the air temperature is warmer.

The problem with the account of Noah's ark and the great flood is the claim of how high the water rose when it was all said and done.

As was mentioned earlier, the higher we get into the atmosphere, the lower the temperature falls.

If we look at atmospheric temperatures, we find that at around 9,000' the temperature is around freezing, or thirty-two degrees Fahrenheit.

At around 10,000' the temperature reaches approximately zero degrees.

This would dictate that moisture above 9000' would begin to freeze and anything above that would only be frozen precipitation.

The average yearly temps at the summit of Mount Everest (29,000'), are around -27 degrees Fahrenheit.

That's about the highest height of commercial airliners at cruising altitude.

At that altitude and temperatures, it would be literally impossible for precipitation to form into a liquid.

In fact, it would be nearly impossible for any moisture above 10,000' to not be in frozen form.

This causes a very difficult problem with the biblical account of Noah's Ark and the great flood because if things began freezing, let's say, even at 10,000', how would it ever be possible to have rain fall above that altitude to flood the earth?

Could you imagine what it would look like if everything was frozen between 10,000' and 29,000'?

There are videos of people in the Northern United States who have taken pots of boiling hot water, and thrown them up into the air on a frigid day where the air temp was around the same temp as the peak of Mount Everest, between -10 to -40 degrees, and every time the boiling water is thrown into the air, it freeze instantly into a "poof" of instant frozen precipitation.

Noah's Ark

This precipitation thrown out of these pans, are similar to the higher ice crystal clouds seen on sunny days.

With the atmosphere being well below freezing, this demonstrates that it would have been impossible for there to have been any water between 10,000' and 29,000'.

There would have been no water for the ark to navigate on!

In fact, in reality, the altitude between 10,000' and 29,000' would be a solid frozen shell surrounding the entire earth.

If the earth had actually flooded and the waters began to rise high in the skies, after about a week and a half of being on the water, Noah's ark would have begun freezing over at around 9,000' due to the temps, much like the crab boats of the Bering Sea, only more severe, and the ark would have likely built up enough ice that it would have sunk, or at best, flipped over due to the added weight on top of the boat.

Most living things on the ark would have frozen to death, including Noah and his family, even before they reached the 40 day mark.

So, it seems that the earth could not have possibly flooded at high altitudes, but rather, would have covered the entire earth with ice and snow, making the entire earth freeze from the outside down through the deep waters into the core of earth.

Imagine how an orange would react in the freezer.

The orange would likely begin at room temp but a soon as it enters the freezer it would begin losing its warm temp, eventually reaching the freezing stage and eventually completely freezing solid.

This frozen condition of earth, high into the skies, would have likely caused a condition to where the earth no longer had an atmosphere, which means the greenhouse effect would be eliminated and the heat from the sun could no longer be trapped in, allowing the freezing temps to take hold and keep hold of the planet, sending it into a long term total earth ice age, only more severe that any the earth has likely seen, due to the volume of ice buildup around the earth, high into the skies, until the sun was able to eventually unthaw it, allowing earth to eventually form an atmosphere once again.

If this were the case, it would have likely taken tens of thousands of years, and more likely, millions of years to melt to the point to which life as we know it, could possibly even begin to exist once again.

So, it Noah and his crew were able to reach the altitude of Mount Everest, it is likely that they would have frozen to death because of lack of proper clothing.

Even if all the people and animals on the ark did not freeze because of the altitude, they would have likely died a horrible death because of the lack of oxygen.

Most of us have seen pictures, videos, or even maybe documentaries of people climbing Mount Everest.

These climbers face hugs challenges, some of which are very deadly, such as low oxygen levels to the point to where if they do not have added oxygen assistance, they could very likely go into comas or even die.

These climbers are very well dressed in the latest high tech clothing to protect them from the extreme colds and weather conditions.

Let's face it, the middle east does not have much use for extreme weather garments.

These climbers struggle at that altitude to do the very basic human functions, such as walking and breathing, which makes it very difficult to reach the summit of Mount Everest, and one of the reasons so many people have died trying to summit Mount Everest.

Now compare that to the account of the ark, and according to the bible, the waters were high above the highest mountains.

See the point here?

Let's say the waters somehow did not freeze at that altitude, the crew and animals would have still had to deal with the lack of oxygen and extreme temperatures.

So, by using logic and facts about what we do know about our planet, our weather system, and our atmosphere, we can prove that the great flood was logically impossible, and if somehow it could have flooded to the height described in the bible, no living human or animal could have survived the temperatures and oxygen levels at the height of 29,000' for the amount of time the Ark was claimed to have been at that level, before the waters receded enough to lower them to a more appropriate temperature and oxygen level.

Noah's Ark

CHAPTER SIX
WHERE'S THE LEFTOVERS?

Let's think about the highly unlikely claim that the earth actually did flood as claimed in the bible, and let's look at the aftermath of the great flood and the receding of the waters, breaking that down to try to see what that might have looked like.

OK, let's say ole Noah and his family were successful in holding onto the boat through the once in a lifetime event, and all the animals managed to survive, and they were all able to make landfall a year later when the waters began to recede, and a bird did not come back notifying the crew that there was dry land somewhere, and they were able to find it.

According to the bible, the water receded steadily from the earth.

At the end of the hundred and fifty days the water had gone down, and on the seventeenth day of the seventh month the ark came to rest on the mountains of Ararat.

The waters continued to recede until the tenth month, and on the first day of the tenth month the tops of the mountains became visible.

OK! Correct me if I am wrong, but, isn't Mount Ararat a mountain, with a top, hence, "mountain top"?

Maybe the bible was referring to Mount Ararat as the "landing place", and all other mountains were considered in the "mountain top" category?

Another question comes to mind regarding the receding of the water: If the earth had as much water as it could hold before the flood, and the waters came from somewhere else to fulfill God's murderous rampage called the great flood, then how would the receding water know to stop receding at sea level?

After all, sea level is called sea level because the waters of earth are at that level and cannot go above or below that level unless water can come from another device, such as "a god" maybe, or maybe even melting ice, to which some say global warming is causing the ice sheets to melt making the sea levels rise, however there has been no evidence of any catastrophic rise in sea levels from that. Only slight variances and manipulative politicians.

If water evaporated and didn't fall back to earth, that may cause sea level to drop, but that would also mean it would be very cloudy all around the world, all the time.

This would cause a devastating greenhouse effect, and then all the ice sheets would melt, and the politicians would for once, then have told the truth.

OK! Moving on!

So, Noah docks the boat, opens the door to the ark, and what does he and the crew see?

First of all, if they landed on Mount Ararat, Mount Ararat is a snow-capped and dormant compound volcano in the eastern extremity of Turkey.

Mount Ararat is the highest peak in Turkey and the Armenian plateau with an elevation of 16,854 feet, and the Little Ararat, has an elevation of 12,782 feet.

Remember the high-altitude temperatures we mentioned earlier in this text?

Going by temperatures that we do know to exist high in our atmosphere, it had to be cold on Mount Ararat, and the waters would have been equivalent to the arctic ocean, if not completely frozen by then, which would have prevented some fish species from surviving, however the penguin and polar bear would have been right at home.

During this time, there would have been no wild plant species available to feed the herbivores, and it would have been impossible to grow any vegetation at that altitude in time to feed them later before they died of starvation.

And according to the bible, it took another three months for the other mountain tops to be visible.

Going at this rate, it would have taken another six to nine months for the water to have receded to close to sea level and close to habitable land.

This causes even more problems because of the effort and supplies that would have been needed to keep all species alive for a longer period of time, and then for the crew to be able to plant every species of plant and cultivate them to the point to where the animals and the crew could have survived long term.

Now, let's pretend that Noah and his family, and all the different species made it through many months on Mount Ararat, with only the supplies and food that was brought on the ark.

When the waters did subside to sea level, what would Noah and his family have seen.

They would have seen all the destruction of the land cause by the great flood.

There would not be a single tree or bush left to use for shade, shelter, food, lodging etc., however there should be plenty of firewood, for heat because of the debris, once it dried out of course.

Noah and his crew would have to climb through and over all the brush and dead human and animal carcasses left over by the storm just to get anywhere.

The ground would be contaminated by all the dead and rotting corps, and their skeletal remains would litter the land.

By the way, Geologist still to date, have not found that dense layer of skeletal remains and vegetation from the great flood, but I'm sure they are still looking! "Wink!"

The carnivore animals would begin eating some of the other species, due to not having anything to eat once they left the ark.

The herbivores would die of starvation due to lack of vegetation to eat.

Noah's Ark

Noah and his family may survive for a little while on some of the animals from the ark, but food would have run out because the larger animals would have eaten the smaller species, and eventually the larger animals would have killed and eaten Noah and his family to try to survive.

And last but not least, one last beast would have been left standing after having defeated and eaten its mate on order to try to stay alive, and then that final beast would have starved to death from lack of food because there would have been nothing left to eat on the planet.

If you could try to imagine a pack of lions feeding on a downed zebra in the wild, and multiply that by thousands of species after the flood.

If you could try to imagine what earth would have looked like compared to the Japan tsunami aftermath of 2011, only worse.

All this destruction and all this carnage and only eight people left to put it all back together. Imagine that!

There would also be an issue because the lack of oxygen on the planet, because plants are very crucial in helping creating oxygen in which humans and animals cannot survive without.

So, without plants to help produce oxygen, Noah and his family and all the animals, would all have eventually died from the lack of oxygen, if they were not eaten first.

There is no other way this story could have actually ended, other than tragically, if Noah and his family and all the different species in the world, were all able to make it through 40 days and 40 nights of rain on the ark, and through almost a year in the mountains before even making it to dry land that would have been washed down to sea level from every mountain during the storm.

All that could have possibly been left would have been some of the marine species and maybe some land water creatures like penguins and seals.

The reason I say some marine species, is because, of the storm and the major disruption of the eco system, and the oceans and waterways of the planet, most of the marine species would have likely perished in the storm, if for nothing else, than all the soot and debris in the water cause by the storm keeping them from absorbing enough oxygen from the water to survive.

This means that, the only life left, which would be bacteria from all the dead bodies, would have to jump start evolution all

Noah's Ark

over again and life would have to come out of the water, once again, populating the earth, as it did millions of years ago.

Who knows what kind of creatures we might become this time?

CHAPTER SEVEN
VEGETATION

Let's think about the earths vegetation and what it would have taken Noah and his family to cultivate and re-vegetate the world after a great flood event.

If the great flood of the bible did actually happen, it is logically clear to see how all terrestrial (land) plants on the planet would have been destroyed, and most of the aquatic vegetation species would have been greatly diminished due to damage from the storm.

This means that Noah and his family would have to load at least one of every species of plant on board the ark, including most aquatic plants, but they would have also had to plant them, after the ark made it to dry land, and pray to their god that the plants survived, which I'm sure theists would claim that God had a helping hand.

Estimates are around a million-different species of terrestrial and aquatic plants on the planet counting catalogued species, noncatalogued species, and subspecies and varieties.

Noah's Ark

As most of us know, it is very difficult to grow plants and vegetation if the proper conditions are not present.

Even if the proper conditions are present, sometimes it is still difficult to successfully germinate and grow plants.

To grow a wide variety of vegetation, which Noah and his family would have done in order to continue all plant species on the planet, would have required a variety of conditions to accomplish this task and to be successful.

Some land plants require more water than others, while other plants may need more sunlight or less sunlight.

Some plants require specific fertilization while other grow easily without special fertilizers.

Some plants only germinate certain times of year whereas others germinate more often.

Some plants such as evergreens, can grow almost everywhere on earth, while other plants such as tropical plants, are explicit to specific regions on earth.

Let's think about what Noah and his family would have needed to do, to begin the process of re-growing the earths vegetation.

When we begin thinking about the rebirth of vegetation on earth after the great flood, it is immediately understood the monumental task Noah and his family would have had in front of them.

The first issue Noah and his family would have likely run into would be, finding enough clear land to regrow the earths new vegetation.

Before beginning this garden of sorts, Noah and his family would first of all, have to clear tons of debris from the land where they planned to cultivate.

As we mentioned earlier in this text, after the great flood, the entire earth would have likely been covered in hundreds of feet of debris left over from the 40-day storm.

All the earth's previous vegetation, every tree, every bush, and every structure on earth would have been washed away by the storms flood waters.

All of this debris would have been left piled up on every bit of dry land on the planet once the waters subsided.

This is not to mention the debris left floating in the waters of the planet, for years to come affecting the eco systems of the planet.

Noah's Ark

Noah and his crew would have needed to clear all of this debris before any plants were planted.

Since Noah and his family did not have great powerful machines to move the debris, and only likely had primitive tools such as axes and maybe handsaws, it would have taken many months to clear enough land to plant just one of every plant species on the planet.

Yes, they could have tried using the two elephants to help pull large objects, but the elephants could not have walked on the debris, and once the crew worked down to the soil, the elephants would have sunk in the wet ground, rendering it implausible to use them.

If we think about this, imagine what that would have looked like when Noah and his family were clearing the land.

Imagine what a river dam looks like after a present-day flood that pales greatly in comparison to the great flood of the bible.

After current day storms and floods, piles of trees and limbs along with other debris end up getting caught on the lip of the dam creating a mound of debris that either has to be removed or over time weakens, breaks apart, and washes on over the falls.

Now, if we take that example and put it in comparison to the devastation of the great flood over the entire earth, Noah and his family would have had to remove mounds of debris from the land in order to plant anything.

Noah and his family would have to begin by pulling the small debris from the area and take it somewhere else to dispose of, and then come back and disassemble the larger pieces of debris, that would likely have been large trees and pieces of structures from buildings that were destroyed in the flood.

This is where they would have to use their axes and or hand saws to cut the larger pieces of debris into smaller more manageable pieces, and then haul them off to get them out of the way so they could plant.

Let's use math to determine what it might take to clear enough land to plant one of every plant species on the planet.

If we gave each plant one square foot to germinate and grow to its entire adult size, it would take a minimum of twenty-one football fields to accomplish that task.

If we do the math, it looks like this: A football field is 100 yards long and 53 yards wide. With a yard being 3 feet, that would equal 300 feet by 159 feet. If we times 300 x 159, that equals 47,700 square feet in one football field.

If we take one square foot for each single plant (1,000,000 species), that would equal 1,000,000 square feet. Now lets divide that by 47,700 feet, and that would equal 20.96 football fields.

With a football field being a little larger than a square acre, that would equal more than 22 acres of debris that Noah and his family would have to remove just to plant one of each species on plant on the planet.

Not only would Noah and his crew have remove the mounds of debris, but once they were able to remove enough debris to get down to the level of the soil, they would have to work in the wet soil, mud, to complete this task, making it tougher and harder to get to and move the larger debris.

Let's pretend that Noah and his family did somehow manage to clear 21 football fields of debris so that they could prepare a field large enough to repopulate the earths entire vegetation pallet. This does not account for many of the plants making it to other regions of the planet, but we will avoid that topic for now.

How long would it have actually taken to plant 1,000,000 different plant species?

If Noah and his family were somehow able to cut, pull, drag enough debris to clear at least one football field of debris a day, that would have taken three weeks, minimum to clear enough land for planting 1,000,000 plant species.

Now after removing all of the debris from the area, Noah and his family would have to wait a couple of days for the ground to dry enough to plant anything because if the ground was too wet, the plants roots would likely have rotted and died, and Noah and his family could not afford to take that risk.

Now if we begin the planting process, by dividing 1,000,000 species of plants out equally among Noah and his crew, that would equal 125,000 plants each person would have to plant to get them all in the ground.

Now, if each person could take one plant per minute, separating them, digging a hole, placing them, and securing them in the ground, properly, it would take each member, nonstop, 24/7, 86 days to get all of the plants in the ground.

That's no breaks, no sleep, no using the bathroom, no eating, etc. for 86 straight days.

That's over double the time they spent slaving on the ark just to keep a million animal and insect species alive!

And, to make things more complicated, these people were hundreds of years old.

Now, if we take the 21 days to clear the land, a couple of days of dry the land, and 86 days planting, that would equal over 100 days the crew would have spent on reintroducing the vegetation of the earth to the soil.

This poses a couple of problems!

Remember the earlier numbers, of Noah's family having to spend so much time caring for each animal on the ark just to keep them alive?

If it took 100 plus days, and every member of Noah's family, every second of that 100 plus days, just to get the vegetation restarted on earth, they would have had to neglect all living animal species on the ark, meaning they would all likely died of starvation and the earth would not have any species besides humans left?

Some theist would likely try to claim that once the ark made it to land the animals could have gotten off the ark and taken care of themselves, which might sound true, but, in actuality, due to the lack of vegetation and habitats, the animals could have not simply just left the ark and survived in the wild after the ark hit dry land.

Where would they go, what would they eat, where would they lodge?

Get the point theists?

In fact, if the story of Noah was true, and the ark did manage to find dry land, it would have been a catastrophic wasteland no matter where the ark landed.

Most land species would have had to remain on or near the ark to be able to survive, and the ark would have had to contain enough food and vegetation for the animals to have survived. That causes an even greater problem with the logistics of the ark as we mentioned earlier. Not to mention that someone would have to help feed the animals while they are still on the ark waiting for vegetation to grow. This would take a substantial amount of time.

So, with the entire crew having to spend 100 days prepping the land and planting vegetation, just to get it in the ground in that short period of time, most species would have died due to lack of food or care.

As we mentioned earlier in this text, because of the storms devastation on every eco system on the planet, Noah would have had to carry most aquatic species on the ark also. So, they would have to be cared for too or else they would have died.

Some theists would likely claim, as a way to make up some time, that Noah and the crew could have put the aquatic species back in the water when they landed, but, with an unstable eco system, most of the aquatic species, would have likely died immediately from shock, so they would have to stay on the ark in their eco-friendly fish tanks, until the waters could have time to settle down, and Noah and his crew could find time to assist in helping recreate the specific eco systems that each fish would need to survive in.

These eco systems would likely have taken years and maybe hundreds or even thousands of years to re-establish enough to be capable of sustaining aquatic life once again.

Another problem with the replanting of all plant species on earth is the time it takes vegetation to grow and mature and produce more vegetation.

Let's say that the herbivores did manage to survive the rough 40 days and 40 nights in the storm, and somehow had enough vegetation on the ark, to eat the 100 plus days that they were unattended by Noah and his family while they were planting the fields.

Once the herbivores left he ark, they would likely have perished quickly, because unless Noah and his family had extra time to plant multiple sets of specific plants for each herbivore species, and unless those plants were capable of growing and maturing fast enough for the herbivores to eat without making them go extinct, which is highly unlikely after only 100 days, the herbivores would have likely eaten all of the available vegetation before it was capable of reproducing enough to sustain a herbivore population on earth again.

Another issue we run into here with the re-cultivation of the earths vegetation, is that, after the great flood, the nitrogen levels would have likely dropped severely, making it even harder for plants to flourish enough to repopulate and grow due to lack of fertilizer (nitrogen) in the soil.

At best, the plants would have grown exceedingly slow, and not fast enough to maintain the diet of herbivores.

Harvesting vegetables and fruits with this deficient soil, would have been almost impossible leaving the crew little to nothing to eat besides the animals that were brought along for the ride.

The lack of fruits and vegetables would have greatly affected the animals and insects that depend on these to survive.

As most of us know, from second grade science class, nitrogen exists in the soil system in many forms and changes easily form one form to another, going in and out of the soil in what we call the "nitrogen cycle."

Plants absorb the nitrogen and once they die, they break back down, releasing nitrogen back into the soil.

In a simplified explanation, the nitrogen cycle is biologically influenced, and without the necessary ingredients (plant waste) the cycle weakens and eventually comes to a halt until conditions are efficient enough to make the cycle work once again.

Biological processes are influenced by the climatic conditions along with the physical and chemical properties of the soil which are important to plant life.

Both the climate and soils vary greatly around the world causing nitrogen levels to vary among specific regions of the planet.

With this information, we can see that Noah and his family would have needed the knowledge to develop a fertilizer immediately after the ark made landfall, and then they would have needed the knowledge to understand how to test the soil, and then create a specific nitrogen friendly environment for each individual plant.

This task alone would have taken a considerable amount of time that the crew and animal species simply did not have.

Another problem with the cultivation of all plant species on the planet is the amount if insects that would have been needed to allow the plants to survive season after season.

There are a variety of insect species that are crucial to vegetation growth and regeneration, with bees being one of the most popular ones.

If the ark carried only two of each insect, chances are that there would not be enough insects to be able to help assist in plant regeneration.

This would leave Noah and his crew the task of manually hand pollinating each pollinating plant on the earth in order to get them to reproduce.

This would have also taken up crucial time that Noah and his family did not have.

Not only would land plants need a lot of help regenerating on earth after the great flood, but aquatic plants would also need the same type of specific care in regenerating in the waters of the earth, so that they could help re-establish the incredibly important eco systems of the planet, which are extremely important to all species on earth, land and aquatic.

With the variety of diverse eco systems on earth, it would have taken Noah and his family years to reproduce them to the point to where they could support the aquatic life within them.

In the meantime, Noah and his family would have spent an enormous amount of time keeping the aquatic plants aboard the ark alive, till such time as they could be reintroduced back into their normal eco systems.

In conclusion to the topic of the vegetation following the great flood, the likelihood that a family of eight could cultivate and regenerate every species of terrestrial and aquatic plant species on earth is absurd even under the most perfect conditions, yet alone the conditions they would have actually been faced with if the flood event was real.

The mere logistics of this task make it literally impossible, and the ages of Noah and his family make it even more impossible.

There are so many issues with the story of Noah, and the topic of this chapter simply being another one, greatly discredits the story of Noah and the great flood, which in turn, weakens the god claim.

Noah's Ark

CHAPTER EIGHT
BOATWRIGHTS

Let's think about the construction of the ark by Noah And his family to see if the story really floats!

One of the biggest issues with the story of Noah and the great flood of the bible is that men who knew nothing about building boats, yet alone a large sea worthy vessels could build such a thing.

The bible says "Make thee an ark of gopher wood; rooms shalt thou make in the ark, and shalt pitch it within and without with pitch. And this is how you shall make it: The length of the ark shall be three hundred cubits, its width fifty cubits, and its height thirty cubits." *Genesis 6:14-15.*

We already determined earlier that the ark was 450' in length, 75' wide, and 45' tall.

During the time of Noah man was only building boats out of hollowed out logs and reeds lashed together to form raft like structures.

Noah's Ark

For a family of eight, who were going to build a 450' boat without and prior knowledge of building a large boat, would be a very difficult challenge at best, and for that same family to have built a boat that size, that could have withstood all the twisting and bending cause by the forces of the huge waves in the storm, 118 times greater than any recorded storm in history, on their first attempt at building a boat, would have been impossible.

The largest wooden ship every built and sailed on the waters, on record, is the Shooner Wyoming, which was 329.5' long and 50' 1" wide, with a draft of 30' 5."

The Wyoming had a volume of 373,054 cubic feet, and after subtracting the volume consumed by the helm and crew quarters and other areas not suitable for cargo, she had a cargo capacity of 303,621 cubic feet. Its deadweight was 6,004 long tons, that is, the weight of the ship fully loaded, including the crew, cargo.

If we take the actual cubic feet of the Wyoming which is 2/3rds the size of the ark, and equivalate those numbers to the size of the ark, that would mean the ark likely only had about 455,431 cubic feet for the crew, the animals, and supplies, not counting plants.

That would lower the amount of space for the occupants on the ark even lower than previously mentioned in this text, from 1.5 cubic feet, to less than a half cubic foot of space (.44') for each species on board.

Because of its extreme length and wood construction, and even though it was enforced with steel, the Wyoming tended to flex back and forth, up and down, twisting in heavy seas, till the long planks twisted and buckled enough to begin allowing sea water to seep inside the vessel.

And, even though the Wyoming had to use pumps to keep its hold relatively free of water, in March 1924, it took on too much water and sank taking the crew with it.

The Wyoming was built by some of the best Boatwright's in the world, with what they thought was a great design, yet still their boat sank because it was not firm enough to withstand the turbulence of the rough waters.

So, to think that the best boat builders in the world were unable to build a wooden boat, 2/3rds the size of the ark, and keep it from sinking, yet four men and four women, who had never built anything of the sorts, with no knowledge of how to build the ark, build a vessel that was bigger than the Wyoming, and withstood the most extreme conditions the oceans have ever known, and their craft managed to stay afloat. Really?

Doesn't sound possible, and in fact, makes absolutely no logical sense.

According to the bible, the ark was to be build out of gopher wood.

If anyone knows what the hell gopher wood is, they might want to pass that on to the biblical scholars so they can make an accurate description of the wood Noah used to build the ark.

There is no such thing as a gopher tree, although gopher wood could be translated as cypress, pine, cedar, fir, teak, sandalwood, ebony, wicker, juniper, acacia, boxwood, slimed bulrushes, and resinous wood. Take your pick theists!

Once again, the bible makes a claim of something that cannot be investigated, so, we really do not know what kind of wood Noah used for the ark.

Another issue with the ark being built as big as the bible claims it was, is the amount of wood it would have taken to build such a structure that could eventually be seaworthy.

Where did Noah and his family get that much wood, and how did they transport it all over the middle east.

The region where Noah was said to have lived, is a diverse geographical area with high mountain ranges along with low laying river and ocean basins, that would have made it very difficult to transport the size of logs that Noah would have needed for the framing and building of the ark.

Not only were Noah and his family, not master boat builders, it would be safe to say that they were not experienced in navigating large water vessels through a terrible storm, or even on calm waters for that matter.

This would be very apparent, and may be the only believable part of the entire story, because even after being in a great storm for over 40 days and 40 nights, the ark landed basically where it started, in Turkey.

And, let's not forget that Noah was an alcoholic.

If you have ever known an alcoholic? They are not very productive, or reliable.

Maybe this is the reason it took one hundred years to build the boat.

So, this leads to a question!

What the hell was God thinking when he chose a drunk man, who had no boat building experience, who was 500 years old, and asked him to build the ark, load the animals, and he and his family would be responsible for repopulating the entire earth, man and animal, after he killed everything else with a deadly flood?

This almost sounds like God was throwing the game and didn't expect Noah to pull it off. Don't you think?

If theists are going to make up any more stories to support their fairy tales, they should at least make them somewhat believable, with some things that could possibly be true in them.

SUMMARY

So, let's think about what we have discussed and summarize the fairytale that we call Noah's ark.

Before the story of Noah, there were multiple stories of several great floods cause by angry gods, who wanted to destroy the human population, with the last great flood occurring about 500 years before the Christian god was created and the story of Noah was born.

When the Christian God came along, he decided to copy what the previous gods had done by flooding the earth, killing everyone but a selected few and some animals, and then depending on these lottery winners to repopulate the entire world to what it is today.

This Christian god picked a drunken 500-year-old man, who had never built a boat, asking him to build the largest boat ever out of minimal supplies from the area, and then to labor on it for 100 years, then open the doors and allow all living species that could walk, crawl, or fly, to board the boat.

Noah's Ark

Eleven species would load the ark every second for 24 hours, and every species (pair of two) would share an average of .44 to 1.5 cubic foot of space, for 40 days and 40 nights, with the crew feeding a minimum of 11 species every second continuously for 40 days and 40 nights, while being tossed and thrashed about the boat in the greatest storm in history with no relief for the entire trip.

God did not even worry about saving the plant life or aquatic species. He decided to leave them fend for themselves during the storm, which didn't work out too good for them because they all died during the storm.

The rain fell at the rate of 6" per minute for 40 days and 40 nights straight, reaching the top of Mount Everest when it was done falling.

During the storm, the rain fell 118 times harder than the hardest rain ever recorded on earth. The rain had to come from outer space because there was not enough H2O on earth to make that much rain, and the rain clouds were unable to produce that much rain, simply because of the ingredients needed to make it rain constantly, for that long, were not available.

Once the rain reached the level of 10,000' it all began turning into freezing precipitation through the remainder of the storm, meaning the earth was covered with 19,000' of ice and snow by the time it reached the top of Mount Everest.

After many months on the waters, the ark landed on Mount Ararat, with the crew and animals having to wait many more months before the nearest mountain tops began to show, then waiting several more months for the water receded to habitable land to where the crew and animals were able to leave the ark.

This land was contaminated by all the dead human and animal corps, along with hundreds of feet of debris from the vegetation that was destroyed and ripped from the lands during the storm, which Noah and his crew, and animals, had to of climb over and through just to leave the ark.

Noah and his sons, and their wives, began trying to have sex to repopulate the world but it was a very difficult task because of their ages and because of inbreeding complications.

Once they were able to conceive and produce children, a majority of Noah and his family's offspring were genetically, physically, and mentally deformed, and god depended on them to continue to repopulate the earth.

Now that I think about it, that could actually explain a lot!

Since vegetation was unable to grow and reproduce fast enough after the crew found manageable land to try to grow on, the herbivores quickly died of starvation because of the lack of vegetation to feed off of.

And since there was no animals available in the wild for the carnivores to feed off of, the carnivores began eating the dead herbivores and other remaining species until they finally ran out of fresh meat to eat.

Eventually, the carnivores turned their appetite towards each other, till their numbers quickly dwindled, which in turn caused them to eventually turn to Noah and his family, because they were the only fresh meat left to eat on the planet.

However, it can be noted, that some of Noah's family were probably lucky enough to have already died of starvation and disease prior to that, because of the lack of food to eat, and the contamination of the entire planet, giving them illnesses that were too great to overcome.

And then, the last beast left standing died, leaving only bacteria to regenerate the earth's population.

Evolution once again has a fresh start!

This story sounds very depressing, but the good news is, it is an obvious fabrication plagiarized by men who did not understand science and math when they authored the story.

The science and evidence, or lack of, is very damaging to the story of Noah and the great flood, which in turn is very damaging to the god claim.

To be able to say the story of Noah and the great flood is a true story, either means you are extremely ignorant, either innocently or intentionally, or you simply do not care if it's true, but you just want to believe it anyways because it would discredit your god's existence if you didn't believe the story.

And if you do still believe the story of Noah, that is a clear sign that you can't live without believing a man-made god who is "helping" you through life, even though, in reality, he isn't!

It's all in your head, as is the story of Noah!

Open your eyes!

Noah's Ark

NOAH'S ARK
LET'S THINK ABOUT THIS

Written by

J. ALAN GROGG

Published by

PUBLISHING

DEDICATION

Noah's Ark

This text is dedicated to people who are able to look at facts and reality, without prejudice, and draw sensible and logical conclusions no matter where it leads.

This text is also dedicated to those who have been brave enough to open their eyes, and question and change their minds about what they have been taught to believe, because of the overwhelming evidence that they have obtained due to their own investigations, which demonstrates that what they have believed for so long, because of being told by others to believe that way, is actually false and dishonest.

It's ok to change your mind and your belief, about anything, especially when you obtain more information that leads you to a different conclusion.

However, it is immorally wrong and dishonest to hold a specific position, at all cost, just because that was what you were always taught, even when there is overwhelming factual evidence to disprove that claim or belief. And, it is even more immoral and absurd, to push false and unjustified claims on others, especially children.

Humans are generally a curious species that have always searched for truth, and by nature, have always investigated everything, but if people have to be told what to believe (religion), then that "truth" was never there in the first place, meaning it has to be fabricated and forced on others, who would have otherwise never believed that "truth", simply because there is no evidence to support that claim and no reason to believe it.

Don't be ignorant! Question everything!